MODERN ENGLISH

TODHUNTER EARLE

INTERIORS

MODERN ENGLISH

TODHUNTER EARLE

INTERIORS

TEXT
HELEN CHISLETT

VENDOME
NEW YORK · LONDON

PREFACE

It seems incredible to us that it is over twenty years since we founded Todhunter Earle. At that time, we both had our own separate design careers and were introduced through a cousin, the fabulous Lulu Fry, who thought we would enjoy collaborating. Ours wasn't a planned partnership, but something gelled. We don't just share a sense of aesthetics – an unspoken understanding of that nebulous term 'taste' – but we also enjoy the same sense of humour and relaxed approach to life.

In those early days, we were a tiny team. Today, our studio numbers around twenty. We run a happy camp, and like to think that this is just one of the reasons why clients feel at ease through a design journey that can be both time-consuming and complicated. Between us we usually work on fifteen to twenty projects a year, spanning a hugely diverse mix of country houses, town houses, chalets, beach properties, yachts, hotels and restaurants. Many of our clients have returned to us again and again, introducing us in turn to their friends and family. We don't impose a Todhunter Earle design signature, but rather respond to each individual property: its architecture, location, period, and how our clients would like to live.

'Modern English Interiors' can be interpreted in a number of ways, but to us 'modern' is synonymous with an understanding of everyday life today. We reference the past when appropriate, but our interiors are also fresh and functional. 'English' is even harder to nail down, but we would define it as relaxed informality, an element of wit, the eclectic combination of old with new, and beauty that sometimes flirts on the edge of scruffiness.

When we began planning this book we were extremely grateful to have so much material to include, because of all the wonderful clients who have brought so many fantastic projects to us over the years and allowed us to photograph and publish them. The truth is we can't believe our good fortune in getting this far, doing the thing we both love and staying friends to boot! We have seen each other through the cliché of thick and thin since our partnership began. And long may it continue.

Emily Todhunter   Kate Earle

INTRODUCTION

When Emily Todhunter and Kate Earle were first introduced, it proved to be a most serendipitous encounter. Today, their interior design partnership is recognised around the world as one of Britain's leading studios. They are one of only a handful of companies to have been included continuously in the Top 100 lists run by eminent interiors publications, lauded both for the breadth of their projects and the ease with which they glide from traditional country to sleekly modern.

By the time they met over twenty years ago, they were each established individually as interior designers. Emily studied Philosophy and Psychology at Bristol University before moving to New York, where she earned a living painting decorative finishes on walls and furniture. Aged only twenty-three, she was retained by Howard Stein to decorate Au Bar nightclub in New York – very much the place to be seen at the time – which put her name on the map and resulted in commissions for several apartments on the Upper East Side of Manhattan. When she returned home to England in 1990, she decorated Nigel Nicolson's private rooms at Sissinghurst Castle in Kent and took on prestigious projects such as the restaurants Daphne's and Christopher's in London.

Kate had a passion for art and design from an early age and went straight into the management of investment flats when she left school. This segued into interior design, and by the age of twenty-one she had set up her own business. At the suggestion of a cousin, she agreed to help Emily with a particularly demanding project for a couple of months, but they discovered such a strong rapport from the outset that it seemed inevitable to continue working together. Although Todhunter Earle was officially launched in 1998, their informal partnership predates it by a couple of years.

Today, they travel across the world, taking on projects that include private residences, ski chalets, boutique hotels, restaurants, private banks and superyachts. Many of their clients return to them again and again, including Raymond Blanc of the renowned Belmond Le Manoir Aux Quat'Saisons. In numerous cases they have come to know the clients so well that they have also become friends. To Emily and Kate, this is one of the best recommendations they could achieve. Discretion being so integral to their business, much of this work has never been photographed, let alone published.

While they have won acclaim for their work on grand heritage houses, they have also undertaken various contemporary buildings as well as new-build country houses with leading English classical architects. What underlies everything they do is a quiet assurance that they can determine elegant solutions in the best taste possible. Underpinning this is a sense of proportion, of something being 'right'. Rather than one object dominating a room, the orchestration of a pleasing composition of colours, textures and patterns is key. There is an Englishness in their approach that is not about chintzy florals, but instead about instinctive design that results in interiors that are relaxed, unpretentious, discreet.

A Todhunter Earle interior whispers, rather than shouts. What is paramount is how the client feels when he or she is in their home. Emily and Kate create rooms that feel loved and lived-in, rather than showy, beginning not with samples and swatches but by spending time with the client, listening to what they say and applying some psychology. How do they want their family to use the space? How will the layout best work for them? How will they experience each room? How will it make them *feel*? It's not about designing houses that look like hotels or show homes; it's about creating places of sanctuary, comfort and delight.

That Englishness is evident not only in their work, but in the way they conduct their business. The Todhunter Earle ethos is 'a happy job is a good job' and although they run a tight ship professionally, their studio – an open-plan office on the top floor of a former warehouse building close to Chelsea Harbour Design Centre – is friendly, buzzing and bohemian. While Emily and Kate typically run up to twenty projects a year between them (although they each head up their own design team, every project that goes out under the Todhunter Earle name has the full approval of both), ranging from light renovation to complete refurbishment, the in-house atmosphere always remains both industrious and full of laughter.

Their creative approach is artistic and highly individual. Often, they will design bespoke pieces – furniture, lighting, fabrics, rugs, even door handles – which then go on to become part of The Emily Todhunter Collection. Their unique way of working is also evident in their longstanding relationship with artist Marianne Topham, whose illustrations are featured throughout this book. These artworks are a collaborative endeavour that is integral to the design process. Both Emily and Kate begin a project by sitting down with Marianne at length, working with her as she translates their ideas onto paper as perspective drawings. Some of these are then coloured for further visualisation. These drawings give a sense of standing in the finished room, and embody a warmth and soul that can only be achieved with a hand-drawn interior. They also highlight design problems at a very early stage, which can then be fully resolved before sharing the final vision with the client. They are an evocative and immediate way of explaining the design intention, and the signed-off drawings are used as a blueprint throughout by every contractor engaged on the project.

From their vast and varied portfolio, achieved over the last two decades and more, Emily and Kate have chosen eighteen private-house projects to celebrate their partnership within this book. Demonstrating both the diversity of their output and the love and care they put into each home they are privileged enough to create, the selection journeys through centuries and across continents, telling the story of each project both in terms of aesthetic inspiration and design solutions to spatial challenges, with that hard-to-quantify Englishness always at the very core.

Having pored over books by their own design heroes (David Hicks, John Fowler, David Mlinaric …) over the years, it is now their turn to inspire others, as they send their first publication out into the world. While they are far too English to pat themselves on the back, this beautiful book is the very best way to do just that.

COUNTRY

SUFFOLK

When Kate met her husband Tom, he came as a package with this Georgian country house near to the Suffolk coast. Originally constructed around 1800 on the site of an earlier house, it was extensively remodelled for the Tollemache family in two separate phases between 1896 and 1914, and it still bears their heraldry in the stone entablature and plasterwork and on the stained-glass windows in the entrance hall. The house may be grand in scale, but there is nothing austere or forbidding about its atmosphere. With its various animals and all the paraphernalia of country living, it is very much a family home to them and their two teenage children.

When Tom bought the house twenty-five years ago, it was evident that time had stood still there since the 1940s. He and Kate met soon after, and the renovation has been a close collaboration between them ever since. Many of the house contents have been acquired by them at auction and local sale rooms, and Kate has some treasured pieces inherited from her grandparents, such as the long-case clock in the hall, a lantern from a Venetian palazzo, a vast still-life, and a figured walnut drinks cupboard.

The principal rooms lead off a sunny central hall, with the dining room to the left and the library to the right. At the other end of the house are the less formal family rooms, which are centred on the kitchen. The first floor mirrors this arrangement, with the master bedroom directly over the drawing room, the spare bedrooms off the main landing, and the children's rooms above the kitchen and family sitting room.

The house is a triumph of marriage, not just of two people, but of two very different tastes. Tom is the more traditional of the two, an enthusiastic collector of all manner of things, including English furniture, portraits, porcelain and books. Kate's tastes are more contemporary, veering towards continental furniture, mid-twentieth-century British art and white ceramics. Happily, they very much enjoy each other's choices and often rehang paintings and move furniture around to accommodate one another's latest finds.

With rooms of such generous scale, Kate has used powdery paint colours and patterned wallpapers to accentuate the high ceilings and original period detailing. However, what matters most to her and Tom are the furniture, pictures, books, objects and hallmarks of family living that have brought the house back to life and made it so warm and welcoming.

SURREY HILLS

This house is a red brick and stone Arts and Crafts villa remodelled from an earlier house, high on a hill and surrounded by trees, with glorious views and flooded with natural light. It is the weekend retreat of a Scandinavian couple with three children; he is from Norway and she is from Sweden, and the brief was to give the house a Scandinavian aesthetic, entirely without the dark antiques and more traditional look often associated with English country houses. The clients brought nothing with them in terms of furniture, lighting, accessories or art. Instead, they asked us to source everything. We scoured international design fairs on their behalf, curating a collection of Scandinavian mid-twentieth-century modern classic pieces by the likes of Josef Frank, Danièle Raimbault Saerens, Märta Måås-Fjetterström and Raoul Ubac, with Rölakan rugs from Ingelstad.

Internally, there was nothing structural to do, other than redesigning the seven large bathrooms, with their wonderful tall sash windows, original shutters and window seats, as well as the kitchen. The challenge was in marrying the architectural features of the Arts and Crafts era with the clients' taste for the pure and the simple. To complement the original painted panelling we chose a cool, neutral palette for the walls, with curtains and upholstery in a blend of linens, wools and velvets. In the drawing room we used unlined dip-dyed alpaca curtains to maximise the extraordinary light from the huge south- and west-facing windows. We left the original timber floors untouched, but added contemporary carpets and rugs, including textured coir in the dining room and wool and silk in the drawing room. The listed status of the house meant that lighting had to be hung from original fixings, so we sourced some eye-catching modern and vintage pieces, including an antique Swedish chandelier for the drawing room and a glass-and-bronze pendant light by Lindsey Adelman to hang over the dining room table.

We think that this is a truly unique and delightfully unusual English country house interior – one that is full of Scandinavian simplicity; never austere, but bringing comfort, harmony and practical glamour to this corner of the English countryside.

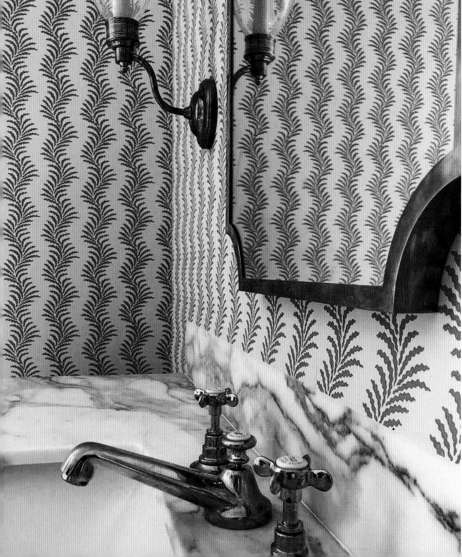

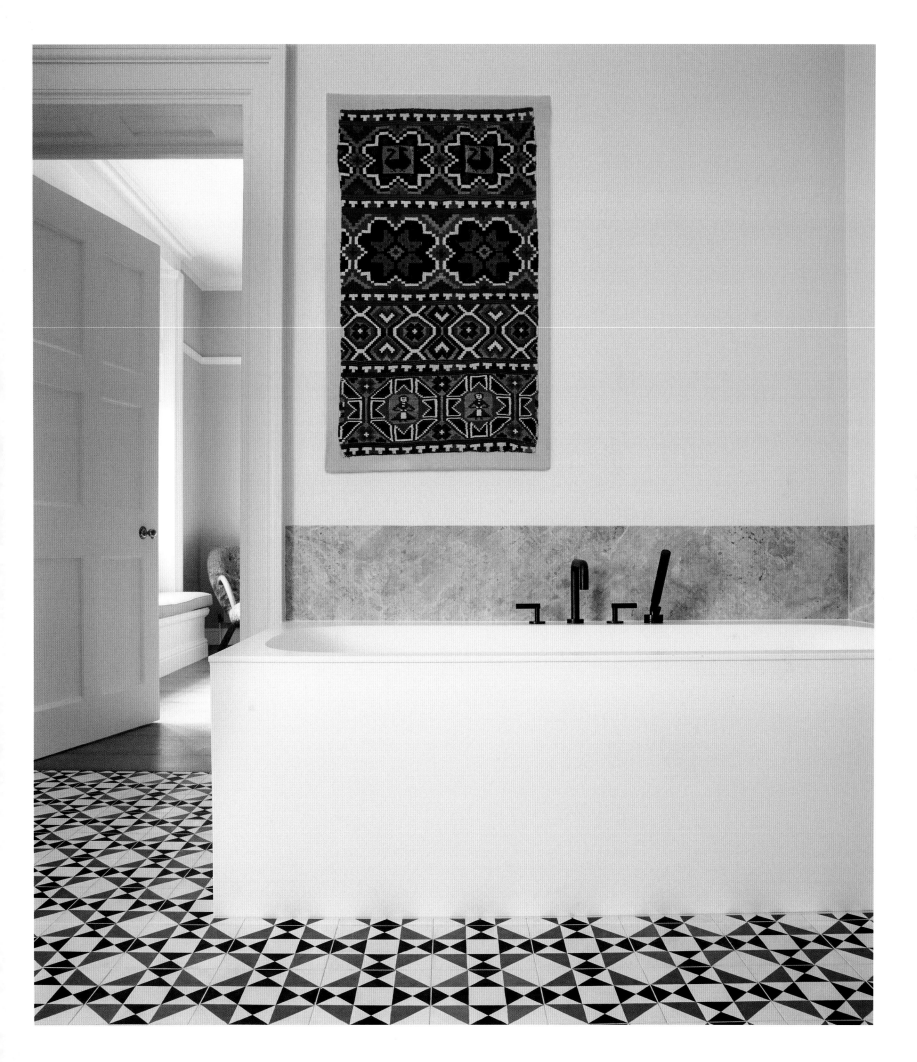

WILTSHIRE

This is Emily's house in Wiltshire that she shares with her husband Manoli Olympitis, their three children, three dogs, and assorted cats, chickens, horses and doves. Originally a farmhouse, it was gentrified in the Queen Anne period, acquiring a classically proportioned brick facade and handsome stone porch. It is an exceptionally pretty house in an idyllic location, but one of the reasons why Emily fell in love with it was because it was relatively untouched, with original sash windows and beams, and fireplaces in nearly every room.

Internally, she has employed a very light touch, avoiding any feeling of the house being consciously designed. Instead, it has been seemingly thrown together, with furniture, fabrics, and floors that can accommodate the mud of country life without fuss. In many ways, it defines the notion of Englishness that lies at the centre of this book: it embraces a relaxed unpretentiousness that engenders a timeless charm, and is a bit scruffy around the edges.

The house is surrounded by a much-loved garden, offering uninterrupted views over the Marlborough Downs. For this reason, curtains are deliberately simple with colours chosen to be soft and unobtrusive, mainly ochres and greens that echo the garden and trees beyond. The original window seats are a feature of the house and have linen cushions that complement the curtain fabrics. For her own bedroom and bathroom, Emily chose a scheme of dusty rose, white and cream, which has a timeless prettiness. Furniture is more hand-me-down than inherited. Blankets cover sofas to protect upholstery from muddy dogs, and books are piled on the dining table. Nothing has been bought specifically for the house; instead, everything gathered here over the years tells the story of the family.

This is the home in which her children have grown up, the family having lived there for fourteen years. It is a sign of how much they love the house that when Emily decided it was time to upgrade the kitchen, she was only given permission by the family to do so if she promised faithfully to install an identical new one.

WORCESTERSHIRE

Overlooking the Malvern Hills, Madresfield Court is one of the most romantic of English country houses. It is the house on which Evelyn Waugh's novel *Brideshead Revisited* is based, and is the ancestral home of the Lygon family, the eldest son of which held the title Earl Beauchamp. The house, its architecture, interior and contents reveal the extraordinary stories of a family that has lived there for almost 900 years. When the latest generation asked us to redesign the interior for their young family, we immersed ourselves in Madresfield's past, so that we could preserve its heritage while bringing this magical, moated piece of history up to date.

Every turn tells a tale, from the bridge over the ancient moat and the arch of the Tudor gatehouse to the courtyard with its Victorian gothic gables and the exceptional Arts and Crafts carvings in the library. Most astonishing is the Staircase Hall, with its crystal balusters designed by the notorious 7th Earl. He embellished the plain chapel that his father had built with romantic murals of himself, his wife and their seven children – a smokescreen for his secret life.

When we first went there, whole wings of the house had been mothballed with furniture covered in dust sheets. The footmen's rooms still had their wig stands and chamber pots by their metal beds. Ivy grew through the windows. Although the house had been inhabited, no children had lived there for nearly a hundred years. There was an air of sadness.

Our first challenge was to reorganise the space, so that it was practical for a modern family of six. We moved the kitchen from its original location to one of the principal rooms overlooking the moat. In all, we redecorated sixty rooms, of which eighteen were bedrooms, emptying storerooms of discarded beds, sofas and chairs that were then repaired and re-covered. Following the path of gentle restoration, we sent paintings and tapestries to be cleaned, restored and rehung. Brighter and lighter colours were introduced into rooms that had long been dust-laden and forgotten.

Three years later, with the help of a talented team and enthusiastic clients, Madresfield blossomed once more. By creating a family home within a stately one, the atmosphere has been uplifted and today reverberates with happiness.

IRELAND

This romantic castle in Ireland belongs to old friends, so when they asked us to help them breathe new life into its interior, we were particularly delighted. Our collaboration has been a work in progress over the last fifteen years or so, tackling different parts of the house in turn.

The castle has been passed down through the same family since it was built in 1614, but when we first became involved in the project it had been many years since it had been lived in by a young family with children. Ireland is beautiful but not exactly known for its sunshine, so we wanted to help create an interior that felt warm and inviting even when it was pouring with rain.

The 'bones' of the house are superb, with eighteenth-century plasterwork, a significant marble mantel by James Wyatt, mahogany doors, original panelling, shuttered windows and oak floors. However, it was tired and in need of revival. The first thing we did was scour the cellars and attics, rediscovering all sorts of things that were then sent for repair and renovation. Unlike many of our projects, virtually nothing was bought for the house.

Structurally, there was little to do other than refurbish the kitchen and the bathrooms. We created a new bathroom for the principal guest bedroom, with a freestanding bath that looks directly out through a tall Georgian window to the lake. As this is such a fine room, with original fireplace, panelling and shutters, we decorated it as we would a sitting room, with armchairs, carpet and armoire.

Rooms as large as this call out for colour and bold use of pattern. On the landing, we chose a yellow that feels uplifting when the skies are grey. In a top-floor bedroom, we took rose-sprigged wallpaper up the walls and over the ceiling. In one of the four-poster rooms we added zest with apple green and white; in another, we chose a riotous pink-on-grey magnolia wallpaper between ceiling and dado.

We have loved playing our part in helping to reshape this magnificent building for generations to come – and it is especially wonderful that we get to stay there and enjoy it, too.

SCOTLAND

This magnificent house in the Scottish Borders had fallen into sad disrepair when our clients bought it. Our challenge was not only to save the fabric of the house, but to transform it into a comfortable and practical home for a family who had been living in Switzerland. This was not just a question of moving house but of moving countries!

Being a listed building, the house required sympathetic restoration, with emphasis on repair rather than replacement. We did, however, manage to gain approval for one significant structural change. The kitchen on the lower ground floor could only be accessed via a dark and narrow servants' staircase. For a young family, we needed the big, renovated family kitchen-come-breakfast room to link to the rest of the house. We extended the main staircase from the hall down through the middle of the house to the lower ground floor. This new layout brings the house together, providing the heartbeat of the home.

When it came to decoration, we were sensitive to keeping as much as we could of the original interior in the formal reception rooms, restoring the characterful old leather that lines the study and colour-matching the very particular shade of green paint in the library. The beautiful sash windows, with views over the countryside, led us to a gentle palette of soft greens, dusty pinks, heathery blues and creams. This is a house that reflects different decorating traditions as well as embracing a European flavour. The master bedroom, for example, is predominantly white and cream, but with antique Dutch furniture set against cool, linen-clad walls.

Weather also influenced our choices. In the borders of Scotland, the wind can be biting, and in winter the snow comes thick and fast. We had to think hard, in particular, about how to make the bedrooms feel like warm sanctuaries. To this end, we used fabric walling in rich colours, wallpapers with cosily enveloping patterns, and thick materials at the windows. Above all else, this has given the house a remarkably welcoming feel.

BELGRAVIA

It is extremely rare to come across a complete property, with original mews house behind, on one of London's most prestigious Belgravia squares. This exceptional project was a case of transforming just such a precious find into a magnificent family house for international clients. At every stage we were commissioned to marry the very highest quality bespoke design with the clients' superb taste in art and sculpture.

We began with a total reconfiguration of the internal space, including digging out three levels below ground to house the swimming pool, gym, cinema, games room, wine cellar and staff quarters. We also built a link between the main house and the mews house behind, where we located the family kitchen. A terrace was constructed on the roof of the new kitchen, connecting the first floors of the main house and the mews. This created a spectacular entertaining area, with the drawing room opening out onto the terrace and leading to the library at the opposite end.

On entering the house, the stairs lie straight ahead with the kitchen beyond. The dining room and powder room are to the right of the stairs. The drawing room takes up the whole of the first floor and the master suite sits above this, with the children's rooms on the third and fourth floors. Having little of the original interior intact, we designed all the internal architectural features, including fireplaces, cornicing, doors and the panelling on the drawing-room walls.

The interior decoration was led by the calibre and impact of the clients' contemporary art collection, which demanded a palette of neutral shades. One of our favourite elements is the bespoke silk runner in ikat pattern that we commissioned for the stairs, which is an artwork in itself.

This was the most incredible commission to work on, but the greatest satisfaction came from knowing we had given the house the status it historically deserved, while also ensuring that it felt inviting and comfortable for a growing family.

KNIGHTSBRIDGE

Although this street is one of London's prettiest crescents, its white stucco houses, with their elegant black railings, are awkward from a design point of view. They are not only tall and narrow, but also slightly wedge-shaped. As an additional challenge, the crescent is on a slight hill, so the garden at the rear is on a different level to the front door.

We had to find ways of maximising space wherever possible, so we created a new basement for the gym, yoga studio and wine cellar, adding a sixth floor to the house. We then had to devise an intelligent way of linking the ground floor – where the kitchen is situated – with the lower ground floor, where the children's playroom leads out to the garden. To achieve this, we shortened the footprint of the kitchen by a few feet, creating a gallery with a glass balustrade that looks down to the playroom. This connects the two floors so that the children can be seen and heard from the kitchen. We then took out most of the back wall and installed enormous double-height doors with glass fins that pivot open to dramatic effect, creating the illusion from the kitchen that you are in the garden – both a functional and impactful solution, ideal for a couple with such a bold, aesthetic sense.

First impressions are important, so we installed timber panelling in the entrance hall, which doubles as a dining room. This traditional solution provides a sense of quiet, warmth and comfort, while the use of pale wood with a horizontal grain added a contemporary twist. Mirrored panels in the hall and on the sliding kitchen doors give the illusion of a doubling of space. In the drawing room on the first floor, the colours are rich and warm – the perfect foil to the clients' sophisticated collection of contemporary design and art. In the bedrooms, we chose a design scheme that is gentler, with the use of velvet upholstery, soft mauvey pinks, silk wallpapers and mirrored cabinets.

This project can perhaps be best summarised as a large scale and rather glorious exercise in successfully manipulating a space to make it seem even bigger than it is.

NOTTING HILL

This Victorian house overlooking one of Notting Hill's famous communal garden squares is a typical London town house. Our clients – a young couple with two small children – had originally been thinking of leaving the city for the country, but ultimately decided they were better suited to staying in the capital. The house was neglected and tired when they bought it, having hardly been touched since the 1980s. Our challenge was to reconfigure all five floors, to transform it into a comfortable and inviting family house, and to return original, internal architectural features.

As with so many houses of this period and location, it is tall and narrow, with rooms of relatively modest dimensions and good ceiling heights. It has the benefit of plenty of natural light, perfect for introducing bolts of colour. In order for us to improve the flow, we opened up the internal spaces. We relocated the kitchen to the front of the house overlooking the gardens, preserving the fireplace within the scheme. The lower ground floor now comprises a spacious playroom, laundry room, and boot room. On the ground floor are the kitchen, morning room and dining room, with the drawing room and study above this, and the master bedroom and children's rooms on the top two floors.

The clients have great taste in art and enjoy collecting characterful, vintage furniture. They also, however, like traditional, English interiors – albeit with a twist. The drawing room, for example, has many conventional aspects that are offset with boldly patterned fabrics and a collection of eclectic lamps. Downstairs, the mood changes to mid-century modern, with Scandinavian prints, pale walls, and accents of mint green and burnt orange. Upstairs, the master bedroom is a blend of classic hummingbird wallpaper and cream linen curtains. The children's rooms at the top of the house are small, but with a clever use of space we managed to include bed, clothes storage and desk in each.

This was a very happy project to take on and we were delighted with the final result: a very English aesthetic imbued with a youthful spirit, resulting in a much-loved family home.

BATTERSEA

The brief for this unique house was to create 'a beach house in the city' for a long-standing client with a gift for finding hidden garden spaces in the most desirable areas of London. When he bought the plot of land, and when we first saw it, it was covered in concrete, weeds and tumble-down garages.

One of the most intriguing aspects about the property is that it is completely unseen from the street of ubiquitous Victorian terraces where it is located. It is accessed via a discreet archway between two houses, which leads to a short driveway. The house is to the left and the garden to the right, but the way that it has been landscaped means the house is almost completely screened by semi-mature trees. It is like walking into an oasis.

We interpreted the 'beach house' brief as light-filled, airy and uncluttered. The front door opens into a double-height hall with cantilevered stairs leading up to the first floor. To the right is the spectacular, double-height sitting room, which is open-plan to the dining room and kitchen. The master bedroom leads off to one side of this and the media room to the other. Upstairs is the library gallery, study and spare bedrooms. We designed the gallery so that the bookshelves appear to continue upwards through the mezzanine floor from the sitting room below. Sliding glass doors allow the house to be completely opened up for entertaining.

When it came to the design palette, we kept everything spare and pure, with no strong colour. The emphasis is on texture, with polished plaster walls, grainy timbers, soft linens and chunky wools. Both house and landscape architecture were designed in tandem, with many of the rooms opening directly to the outside. This inside/outside aspect of the house is integral to its character, with rills of water stepping down towards the house, reflecting trees and sky.

Although we envisaged the finished house from the planning stage, it was truly exciting to walk in for the first time, once it had been completed, and actually experience it. We are very proud to have created such a hidden gem of peace and solitude, just a stone's throw from the uniform streets of terraced houses in this part of south London.

EARLS COURT

Our challenge with this house was to meld the tastes of our clients – a couple who would freely admit to being, in many ways, polar opposites. To complicate matters, the house belonged to him before they met. It was charming, in a dated way, but the kitchen was in the basement. This felt dark and removed, and did not suit her – a talented and passionate cook.

The house is surprising for central London. Long and narrow, it is a 'barn in the city', built over several former gardens and found by walking through a gate in a wall. We turned the layout upside down, repositioning the kitchen and living areas in one huge open-plan space on the first floor. The kitchen, galleried with a glass balustrade, now has views directly over the garden and is connected to it by just a few steps. We removed the whole of the back of the house and installed enormous windows and sliding glass doors. This flooded the kitchen with light, making it feel like an extension of the garden. We also replaced the single central staircase with two new staircases at either end of the house, which vastly improved the overall circularity and flow.

The next challenge was to create a space in which both of our clients would feel happy. Previously, he was used to traditional interiors and was unsure whether he would feel comfortable in the cleaner, cooler space that she envisaged. As with so much of interior design, this was a balancing act; the rooms now reflect both of their characters. Warm colours and textures – including cherry-red velvet walling, inky-blue boarding and stitched leather handrails – counteract metal and glass. During the project they discovered a shared passion for collecting contemporary art, and enthusiastically embarked on the process of commissioning the magnificent water feature sculpted by Jordi Raga that dominates the inner courtyard.

We see it as a testament to the success of the project that the couple married before the house was completed, crediting us with finding the harmony of styles that works for them both.

CHELSEA

We particularly love working with these clients because of their very English wit and personality, mixed with an impressive streak of bravado. This was an unusual project, as it involved taking two typical London terraced houses and knocking them into one, creating a family house for our clients and their three children. Together with the architects and structural consultants, we took the opportunity to rethink the whole space entirely.

To avoid walking into the usual narrow terraced-house hallway, we opened up the entrance area to become a room with a fireplace and a personality of its own. Leading off the hall are the study and the drawing room, which span the whole rear of what was formerly the two separate houses. Outside the drawing room we added a generous veranda with an awning and heating. At any time of the year, the doors can be flung open, effectively doubling the feeling of space.

The stairs were typical of this style of house, so to ring the changes we stripped out the dado rail and installed panelling on one wall of the staircase from the top of the house to the basement. Painted in a strong grey-green, this makes the staircase practical in a house with children, as well as providing a visual connection linking each floor.

Downstairs, the sleek timber-and-marble kitchen is open-plan to the dining room. The latter leads straight out into the garden through wide, sliding glass doors. Below this is a new basement level accommodating a media room and the boys' bedrooms. We configured the house so that the garden can be accessed from both of these floors as well as the ground floor.

We had huge fun choosing fabrics and wallpapers with our clients, including the monkey-print curtains in the hall and study and the gilded bamboo on the ceiling of the downstairs cloakroom. These quirky touches are balanced with elegant finishes – aubergine velvet on the walls of the dining room and raw silk in the hall. Colours are rich, including warm oranges with bitter yellows and mint greens combined with hot pinks. Like the clients, the house is a winning combination of cool and comfort; the unexpected and the unpretentious; of sophistication and moments of silliness. It was a joy to help them create a home that fully reflects their taste, humour and individuality.

CASPIAN SEA

This contemporary beach house belongs to loyal clients who split their time between London and this property on the Caspian Sea. Nothing in this house is ubiquitous or standard: this really was a project that demanded we pushed the boundaries at every stage.

The scale of the property is huge – ideal for the clients' largest pieces of modern art and sculpture – with numerous buildings in which we had a hand. In addition to the main house, these included a cabana on the beach, the pool house, a guest cottage, a sports pavilion, staff accommodation, and a variety of gazebos, potting sheds and glasshouses.

In the main house, one elevation has full-height sliding glass doors that lead out to the infinity pool and beach beyond. The weather in this part of the world can be very hot but also windy, so we had to ensure that nothing would move or rattle.

Our challenge was in finding a way of softening the lines and breathing warmth into the spaces without diminishing the modern architecture. In the dining room we used abaca rugs and commissioned de Gournay hand-painted willow design wallpaper and semi-transparent silk organza curtains. In the kitchen the incredible ceiling heights meant that we could bring texture by using a combination of stucco plaster walls containing mica together with embossed ceramic tiles. For the living room, we commissioned a carpet of vintage saris, adding contrast with woven leather and silk walls. In the hall we used enormous carved wooden panels by Etienne Moyat to punctuate the space between the entrance and reception rooms. The region has bright, white light, inspiring us to introduce elements of strong colour, such as cobalt blue and a mimosa yellow in the children's rooms.

We designed the outside spaces as individual rooms, too. Texture is again the driving force here, seen in the patinated copper finish of the pool house fire surround, slatted wooden ceiling, resin-and-timber table and coir carpet.

This was by far the biggest, most complex and lengthy international project we have undertaken to date, and it was an absolute privilege to see it take shape from conception to completion over the course of four years or so.

When we first saw this handsome, almost fairy-tale, château in France, the building had long fallen into neglect and disrepair. Unmodernised and left as an empty shell open to the elements, its floors were essentially each one cavernous room with original beams and hints of the original stonework, joinery, and floor tiles. The owners – an international couple (she is American; he is French) – had asked us to transform this inherited property into their country family home.

The oldest part of the house dates back to the eleventh century and, as with most period buildings in the Loire Valley, it is protected as a *monument historique* under French law. This required us to follow strict guidelines, including no permanent partitions internally and no services placed within the preserved structure of the building. We resolved the wiring with an infra-red system, negating the need for conventional chasing of cables. We also devised a way of configuring the space on each floor by constructing boarded-timber box partitions through which to run the plumbing without damage or disturbance.

One of the advantages of working in France is that each artisanal trade is highly specialised, so the work is of superb quality. This enabled us to restore period features and build upon them with a modern twist. As the château has such wonderful original oak beams and medieval stonework, we designed the interior to be rustic in character, with oak joinery, roughly plastered walls, original terracotta-tiled floors, large pieces of antique furniture, and a plaited leather banister rope on the stone stairs.

Access for the installation of furniture was an issue, as the spiral staircase connecting the main entrance to the two upper floors was too narrow to accommodate most pieces, let alone larger items such as beds or chests of drawers. Once all building work was completed, we temporarily removed the stone mullions from a large window on each floor and craned in all pieces of furniture that could not pass via the stairs.

This was a project filled with challenges, but the end result was an interior that is contemporary and yet in harmony with the original fabric of a beautiful building of historic significance.

SARDINIA

We always love it when clients return to us with a new project. This spectacular Mediterranean island villa is one such example: existing clients for whom we had designed a London house bought a piece of land on the island and commissioned us to work alongside their architect to design their dream getaway.

Given the many planning restrictions on Sardinia, this building – constructed from local stone and wood – was sympathetically designed to merge ingeniously with the sloping volcanic landscape along this stretch of the coast. The brief was that every room should face the sea. The rooms seemingly tumble down the hill with no straight lines in evidence, while the heavenly pool fits naturally into the contours of the rocky landscape. We advised on the layout of the interior and exterior, to help find a solution that would create a balance of living space and private sanctuary; of inside and outside.

Because of limitations on the internal square footage allowed, generous verandas or terraces were created for each room. The sitting room, for example, doubles in size once vast sliding doors are opened out to the terrace beyond. The bedrooms are quite modest in proportion, but each has its own private terrace complete with bamboo roof and daybed.

A fine dust blows up the rocks from the coast, so everything had to be practical and easy to clean. We chose predominantly natural materials – wood, tiles and stone – sourced from the island where possible, with outdoor rugs and fabrics. Colours reflect the sea, but also the ochre shades in the rock. Plaster is the key finish here, both in the way it has been used to sculpt niches, shelves and furniture into the fabric of the house, but also in the poured, polished plaster of the floors that feels so soft underfoot. With no room for cupboards or wardrobes, simple linen curtains are hung over space hollowed out from the plaster. It was a light touch of beautiful simplicity that perfectly suited this idyllic island home.

ST. MORITZ

This apartment was originally two penthouses designed by Sir Norman Foster overlooking the Saint Moritz lake: a glass box built on the roof of a period building and benefitting from fabulous views over water and mountains. We wanted to create a very particular look – one that works with the clients' contemporary art collection and the modern architecture of the apartment, yet also gives a nod to traditional Alpine style and design.

In order to transform the space into one huge apartment we designed a layout similar to an H-shape, with an open-plan living/dining room looking out over the lake to the front, mirrored by the same spatial footprint to the rear, where the master bedroom is located. Our clients wanted us to give the interior a warmer mood, more in keeping with their family life, so we clad one wall in each room with timber boarding, using the beauty of natural wood to introduce character and texture. Most of the scheme is simple and tonal, with cashmere curtains and walling, and flat-panel doors that seem to disappear. Pattern adds an additional layer of comfort, such as the indigo carpet we commissioned for the living room, the repeating motif inspired by a seventeenth-century Italian document.

Russet reds provide contrast, both on cushions and the leather wall of storage in the dining area. We also chose a variety of natural textures, including cowhide, horse-hair, velvet, linen and vintage Fortuny fabrics. In the master bedroom and dressing room, we bordered the curtains with the subtle accent of bespoke embroidery.

Working in Switzerland is a great pleasure, because everything runs so very efficiently. There are, however, also strict rules about when building work can be done, so that noise and disruption are kept to the minimum during the popular winter season. Our clients were determined to spend Christmas here, and we not only managed to meet the deadline, but also decorated the Christmas tree for them – complete with a heap of wrapped presents – before their arrival. We were delighted that they were thrilled with their new winter retreat.

SAILING YACHT TWIZZLE

Twizzle was a truly ground-breaking project – a magnificent 57.5-metre (188-foot) sailing yacht, built by Royal Huisman in Holland, on which we collaborated with Dubois Naval Architects and Redman Whiteley Dixon (RWD). We had already worked on the clients' motor yacht, so were delighted when they asked us to take on the interior design of Twizzle.

From the first, we established datum lines dictating the height and proportions of the furniture. Our mantra was that we should simplify as much as possible, allowing the eye to settle and relax. In practical terms, this meant keeping heights of furniture aligned. Beds are level with bedside tables, sofa seat heights and coffee tables, and sofa backs are the same height as headboards. This considered design language brings coherence to the scheme, creating a look that is sleek and elegant. The cabinetry is executed perfectly, with furniture wrapping around the space flawlessly.

We wanted to create interiors that would blend imperceptibly with the cool, contemporary finishes of the exterior. RWD had specified a very pale timber for the decks, which we continued through the main salons and echoed in the internal finishes. Glass partition walls allow the eye to travel unhindered through the adjoining rooms. Colours are warm and quiet – coffee shades that range from milky latte to espresso. Everything is tactile and speaks of quiet luxury, while engendering a comfortable, relaxing mood.

Because the concept was calm and uncluttered, the clients did not want conventional artworks, but neither did they want to leave walls bare. Instead, we designed and commissioned large embroidered panels that add interest and character. We used fabric walling in cabins, minimising sound and creating a feeling of being safely cocooned. Soft furnishings adapt far better to a yacht setting than people often imagine, as high technical specifications ensure the atmosphere is never damp.

Twizzle won many awards, including Best Interior Design, Best Superyacht Interior Design, and Best Sailing Yacht Design from the International Superyacht Society (ISS). However, from a personal point of view, this was undoubtedly one of the most fulfilling projects we have ever worked on – a true collaboration with so many talented people. Happiness and positivity seem to run through every aspect of the design, resulting in a yacht that is still turning heads.

VERBIER

To put it simply, there are two ways to approach designing a ski chalet: either to embrace the view, with huge windows and a neutral scheme, or to create a traditional, cosy retreat in which to hunker down after a day on the mountain. This chalet in Verbier was in need of a major overhaul, and our clients preferred the more traditional route, as it was essentially going to be a place where they wanted to have fun. They also needed more space for friends to come and stay, so came up with the idea of moving a *mazot* (small farm building – in this case, a cow shed) from a nearby farm to become a self-contained guest cottage.

In both the main chalet and the *mazot* we used untreated timbers, local stone and linen curtains on the typically small windows. We introduced warm, tactile fabrics at every opportunity – moleskin on sofas, imitation zebra skin on the desk chair, fur throws on the beds and horsehair on the bedheads. Antique painted furniture and boldly patterned cushions helped to amplify the look and feel.

We brought in an element of the unexpected, too. The dining table has a wonderful tree-trunk base and wrap-around zinc top, with a chandelier made of bone hanging above. The russet coffee table is a patchwork of textures: hair-on-hide, leather and suede. It is also strong enough to dance on – something our clients specifically requested! A side table by Fredrikson Stallard appears to be nothing but a simple bundle of logs tied together. The base of the standard lamp has been made from upcycled skis, while a quirky collection of vintage ski posters replaces traditional artwork.

The *mazot* was an exercise in space efficiency, as it is a minuscule one-up, one-down. Downstairs, we just had room for the L-shaped red sofa and television. Upstairs, we solved the problem of where to put the bathroom by integrating it into the bedroom. The WC is hidden behind a tall mirrored door.

Outside, on the terrace, there is an inviting fireplace with a traditional stone chimney, surrounded by armchairs and sofas with generous cushions and rugs covering their solid stone frames.

This is an all-year-round chalet, designed to be unpretentious, comfortable and lots of fun. It makes you smile from the moment you arrive.

ACKNOWLEDGEMENTS

There are lots of people we would like to thank for all they have done for Todhunter Earle over the years. To all of our clients – big and small, past and present – thank you for putting your trust in us. To all of those who have been part of the Todhunter Earle team since the very beginning – thank you for all your hard work, support, inspiration and dedication. We couldn't do what we do without you. To Marianne Topham, a huge thank you for the incredible work that you do with us and for allowing us to reproduce just some of that work in this book. To Helen Chislett, we owe particular thanks for helping us to get this book off the ground and for providing the wonderful text. To all the photographers we work with, most especially Ray Main and Paul Massey, thank you for interpreting the interiors we create so beautifully.

And finally, a big thank you to David Shannon and Beatrice Vincenzini of Vendome, Roger Barnard of Velvet Design and Lucy Henson for making the bringing together of this book so much fun.

COUNTRY **SUFFOLK** (*Pages 18–33*) Architect: Nicholas Jacobs Architects. **SURREY HILLS** (*Pages 34–47*) Architect/Contractor: Managed By. **WILTSHIRE** (*Pages 48–63*) Kitchen: Orwells Furniture. **WORCESTERSHIRE** (*Pages 64–75*) Architect: Donald Insall Associates; Kitchen: Jane Taylor Designers; Lighting: John Cullen Lighting. **IRELAND** (*Pages 76–93*) Collaborator: Serena Williams-Ellis.

TOWN **BELGRAVIA** (*Pages 112–125*) Architect: Adam Hunter/Finchatton; Cabinetry: Kaizen Furniture, Gosling. **KNIGHTSBRIDGE** (*Pages 126–139*) Architect: PTP Architects London; Construction: Cordles; Cabinetry: Kaizen Furniture; Garden: Guy Thornton. **NOTTING HILL** (*Pages 140–151*) Architect: Flower Michelin. **BATTERSEA** (*Pages 152–161*) Architect: BLDA; Cabinetry: Kaizen Furniture; Garden: Osada Design. **EARLS COURT** (*Pages 162–175*) Architect: Flower Michelin; Kitchen: Orwells Furniture; Lighting: John Cullen Lighting; Garden: Tania Compton. **CHELSEA** (*Pages 176–187*) Architect: Icon Architects; Kitchen: Holloways of Ludlow; Garden: Cameron/GN Landscape Design.

ABROAD **CASPIAN SEA** (*Pages 190–201*) Architect: Erginoglu & Calislar/Studio Indigo; Lighting: Lighting Design International; Garden: Scape. **PAYS DE LA LOIRE** (*Pages 202–211*) Lighting: Lighting Design International. **SARDINIA** (*Pages 212–227*) Architect: Luca Aureggi Westway Architects. **ST. MORITZ** (*Pages 228–241*) Architect: Küchel Architects/Studio Indigo; Lighting: Lighting Design International. **SY TWIZZLE** (*Pages 242–253*) Architect: Dubois Naval Architects; Construction: Royal Huisman; Collaborator: Redman Whiteley Dixon; Lighting: Lighting Design International. **VERBIER** (*Pages 254–269*) Architect: Philippe Vaudan Architecture.

ART CREDITS **BELGRAVIA** (*Pages 116–117*) © George Condo/DACS. **KNIGHTSBRIDGE** (*Pages 128–129*) © Julian Schnabel/DACS; (*Page 133*) © Damien Hirst/DACS; (*Pages 136–137*) © Joan Miró/DACS. **EARLS COURT** (*Page 166*) © Marzia Colonna; (*Page 170 br*) © Lynn Chadwick; (*Page 171*) © Merete Rasmussen; (*Page 174*) © Jordi Raga. **CHELSEA** (*Pages 178–179*) © Tom Hammick/DACS; (*Page 181*) © Chris Levine. **CASPIAN SEA** (*Pages 192–193*) © Eric Fischl/DACS; (*Page 196*) Knife Installation © Farhad Moshiri. **ST. MORITZ** (*Pages 232–233*) © Andy Warhol; (*Pages 236–237*) © Rebecca Warren; (*Pages 240*) © Garth Weiser; (*Pages 241*) © Cindy Sherman; (*Pages 256 & 266*) © Fredrikson Stallard.

First published in 2021 by The Vendome Press
Vendome is a registered trademark of The Vendome Press, LLC.
www.vendomepress.com

NEW YORK

Suite 2043,
244 Fifth Avenue,
New York, NY 10011

LONDON

63 Edith Grove,
London,
SW10 0LB

PUBLISHERS

Beatrice Vincenzini, Mark Magowan & Francesco Venturi

Distributed in North America by Abrams Books
Distributed in the UK, and rest of the world, by Thames & Hudson

ISBN: 978-0-86565-393-1

EDITOR Tessa Monina
PRODUCTION DIRECTOR Jim Spivey
CREATIVE DIRECTOR Roger Barnard

Library of Congress Cataloging-in-Publication Data available upon request.
Printed and bound in China by 1010 Printing International Limited.

FIRST PRINTING